CHARTING
THE CLASSICS

CLASSICAL MUSIC IN DIAGRAMS

CLASSIC *f*M

First published 2014 by
Elliott and Thompson Limited
27 John Street, London WC1N 2BX
www.eandtbooks.com

ISBN: 978-1-78396-099-6

Copyright © Classic FM Ltd 2014

9 8 7 6 5 4 3 2 1

A catalogue record for this book is available from the British Library.

Design and illustrations: Jon Wainwright, Alchemedia Design

Printed in Slovenia by DZS Grafik

Introduction

Every day on Classic FM, we're lucky enough to broadcast the world's greatest music to our millions of listeners up and down the UK.

As well as playing brilliant recordings of the finest examples of the genre, made by the greatest soloists, ensembles and orchestras, we're always on the lookout for other ways to share classical music that are slightly different and rather more offbeat.

So, for this brand new book, we decided to take some of the best-loved pieces of classical music and to present them as a collection of mathematical diagrams and charts that you might more normally expect to see as part of a business presentation.

There has long been a connection between classical music and mathematics, and there's no better example of this than the composer Johann Sebastian Bach. He was fascinated with all things numerical, particularly the number 14. The attraction to these digits came after he gave each of the letters in his surname a number depending on where it comes in the alphabet. You'll find references to 14 in many of his musical works.

There's no right or wrong way to read this book, but each diagram illustrates a different classical work. You can check out the full list of which classical work is on which page in the index at the back.

We broadcast the classical charts every week on Classic FM, based on sales of classical music CDs and digital downloads, so it's been a novel experience for us to create charts that involve reading, rather than listening. We hope that you have as much fun looking at them as we have had in putting them together.

Suitable building sites for Jerusalem

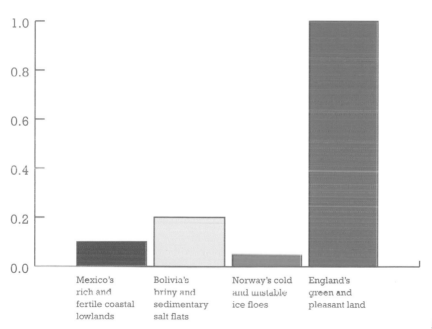

Scale of terrain/precipitation pairings in Scotland

Eric Carmen/Rachmaninov crossover indicator

Hungry Eyes
Make Me Lose Control
Love Is All That Matters
She Did It
Never Gonna Fall In Love Again
Change Of Heart
I'm Through With Love
It Hurts Too Much

All By Myself
Piano Concerto No. 3

Rhapsody on a Theme of Paganini
Etudes tableaux
The Miserly Knight
Piano Concerto No. 1
Piano Concerto No. 2
Russian Rhapsody
Two Don Juan Episodes
Symphony No. 3
Symphonic Dances

Possible mountains for overnight stay

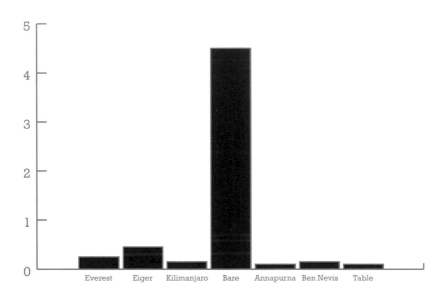

Typical Mussorgskian character traits

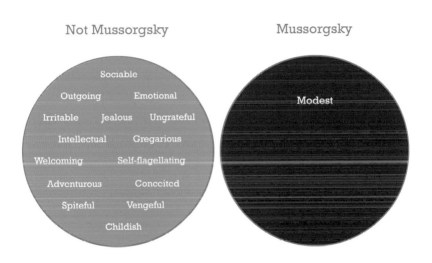

Bach's preferred clavier character traits

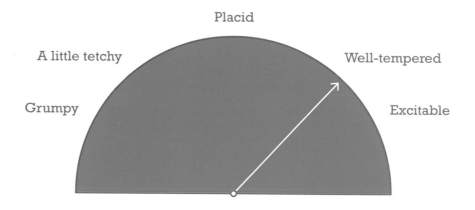

Placid

A little tetchy

Well-tempered

Grumpy

Excitable

Holst's party guests

GUEST	BRINGS
Mars	War*
Venus	Peace*
Jupiter	Jollity
Saturn	Old Age
Uranus	Magic set
Neptune	Crystal ball

*Don't let them sit together

Requirements for entry into Elgar's land

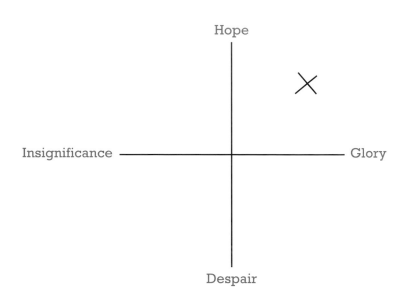

Responsibility for the anointment of King Solomon

How Prokofiev loves to eat five a day

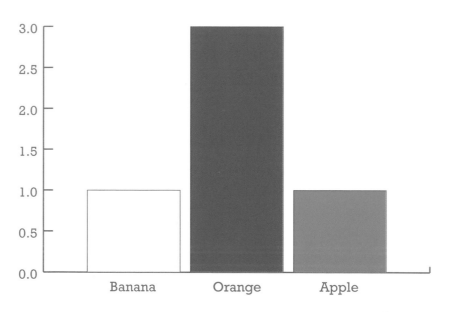

John Philip Sousa's guide to fashion

Polkadot _____ out

Paisley _____ too sixties

Stars and Stripes _____ forever

Plaid _____ so last year

John Cage's 4'33"

Ornithologist's report:
Bizet's favourite wild birds

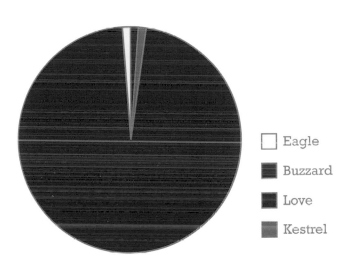

- Eagle
- Buzzard
- Love
- Kestrel

Birds most likely to receive an ASBO

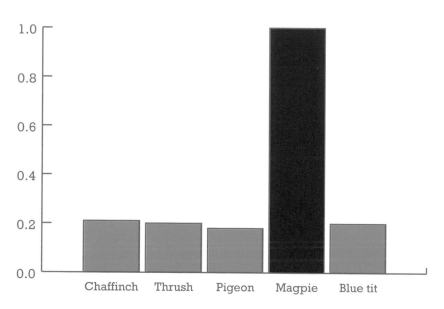

Minimalism: projected musical results

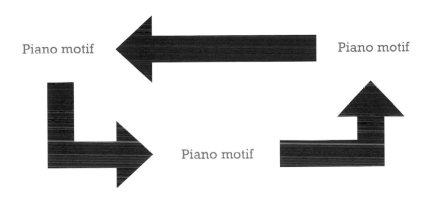

Ratio of Fa:La when decking the halls

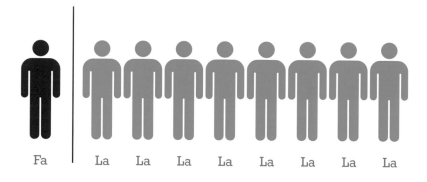

Number of corners required in composer millinery

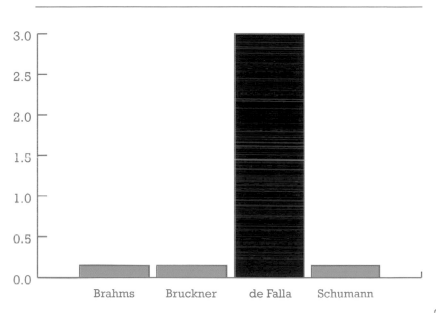

Piracy origins in classical music

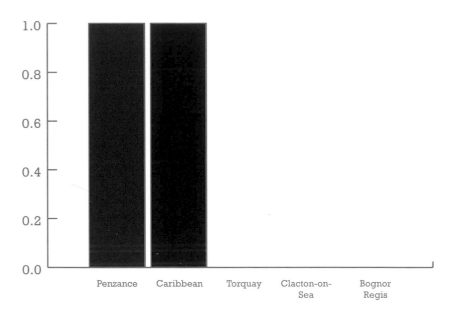

Unforgettable years in
the early 20th century

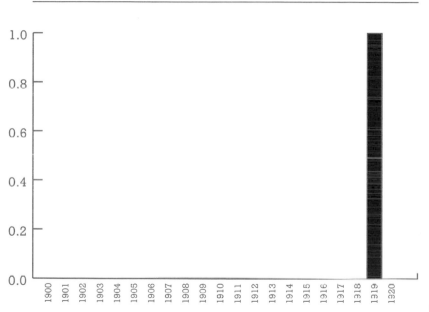

Classical music quality guide

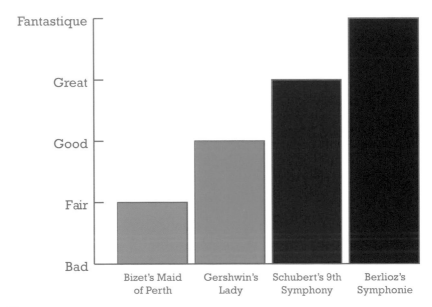

Presence of Gershwin's fellow countrymen in European cities

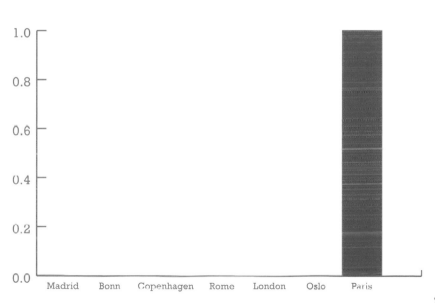

Mythical creatures schedule

DAY PLANNER

AM		PM	
12:00	*TROLL*	12:00	*FAUN*
1:00		1:00	
2:00		2:00	
3:00	*MINOTAUR*	3:00	
4:00		4:00	
5:00	*OGRE*	5:00	*CENTAUR*
6:00		6:00	
7:00		7:00	
8:00	*GNOME*	8:00	*DRAGON*
9:00		9:00	
10:00	*PIXIE*	10:00	
11:00		11:00	

(11:45 – Prelude)

ABBA albums owned
by the Queen of Sheba

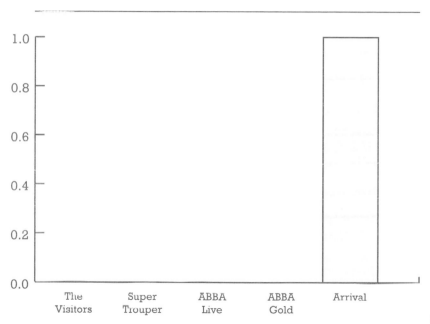

Shining things beloved of Eric Whitacre

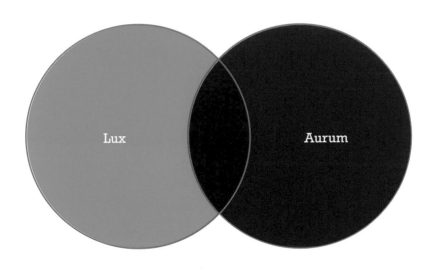

Lux

Aurum

Market share of banks in classical music

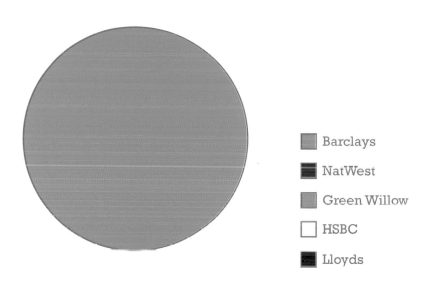

- Barclays
- NatWest
- Green Willow
- HSBC
- Lloyds

Forces required for Mahler symphonies

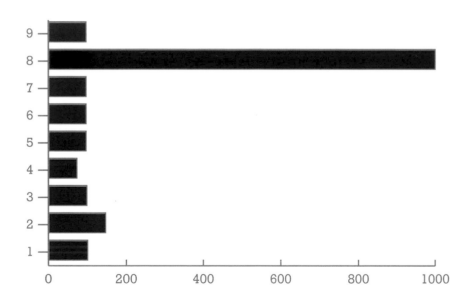

Prospective colour chart:
Gershwin residence

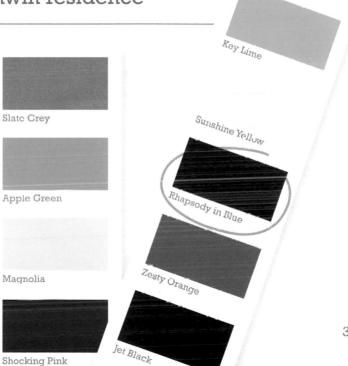

Key Lime

Slate Grey

Apple Green

Magnolia

Sunshine Yellow

Rhapsody in Blue

Zesty Orange

Shocking Pink

Jet Black

Optimum time of day
to make an overture

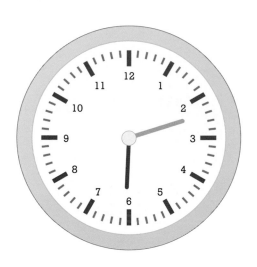

Weapons checklist for Pachelbel

- ☐ Dagger
- ☐ Pistol
- ☐ Musket
- ☑ Cannon
- ☐ Rifle
- ☐ Machine gun

Analysis of hotel stays by Antonio Vivaldi

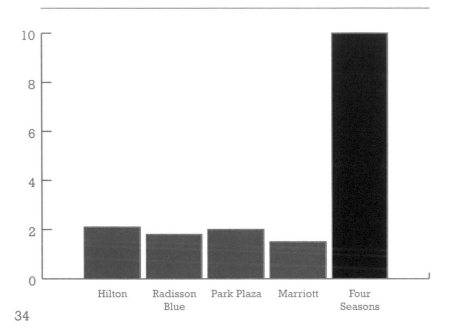

Record of catch by operatic fishermen

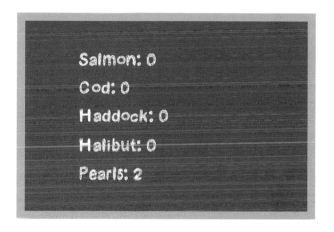

Guide to Parry's mood

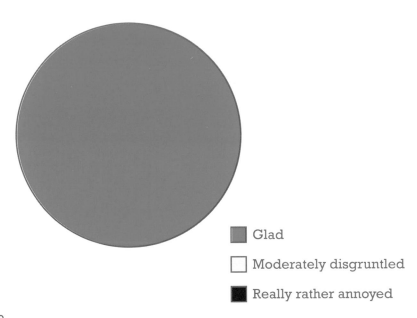

■ Glad

☐ Moderately disgruntled

■ Really rather annoyed

Actions in the event of seeing the conquering hero coming

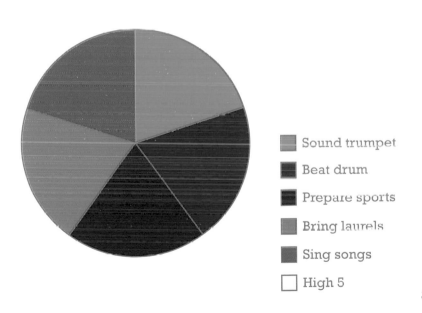

Sound trumpet

Beat drum

Prepare sports

Bring laurels

Sing songs

High 5

Ideal ingredients for an Elgar march

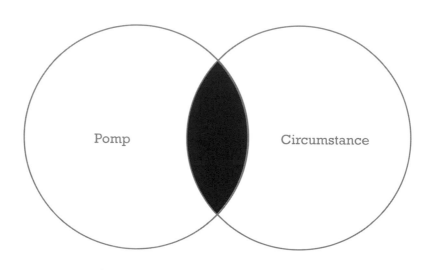

Five variants of Dives and Lazarus

1. Saliva and Dr Zeus

2. USSR and Diva Zeal

3. Viz Salad and Asunder

4. Save us and Lizard

5. Sus Dada Zen Rival

Recommended locations
for John Barry's music

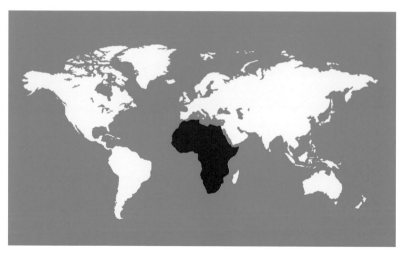

☐ Recommended   ■ Not recommended

Propensity for woodwind instruments to take on magical properties

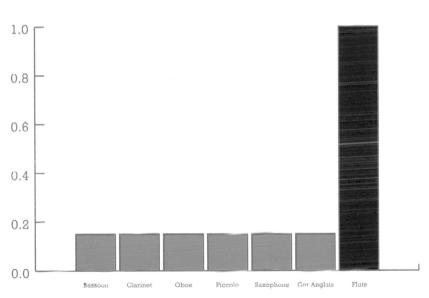

Modes of transport to the Paradise Garden

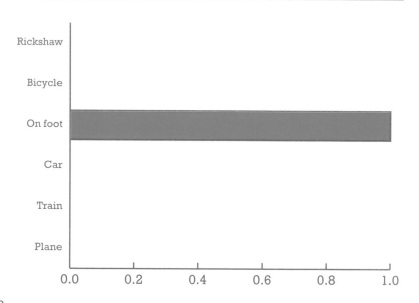

Mendelssohn's summer appointments

			June			
Sun	Mon	Tue	Wed	Thu	Fri	Sat
1	2	3	4	5	6	7
8	9	10	11	12	13	14
15	16	17	18	19	20	21
22	23	24 *(DREAM)*	25	26	27	28
29	30					

Important considerations upon being laid in earth

- ☐ Where
- ☐ Why
- ☐ What
- ☑ When
- ☐ Who

Breeds of penguin favoured by Beethoven

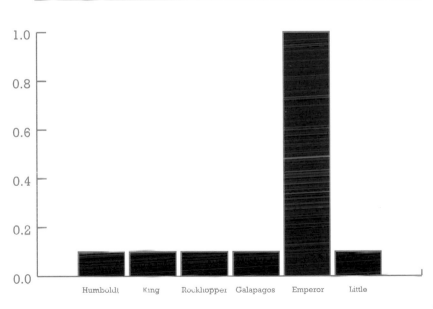

Dvořák's wine list

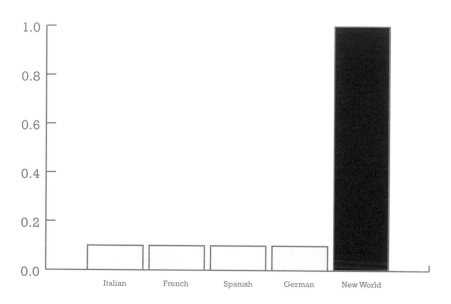

Types of underwear common to Bach airs

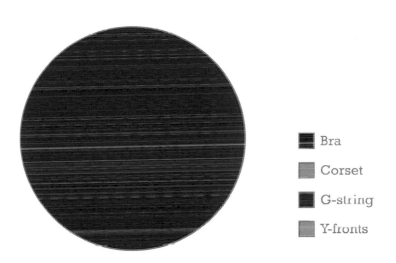

- ■ Bra
- ■ Corset
- ■ G-string
- ■ Y-fronts

Timeline for composition of Haydn's Symphony No. 94

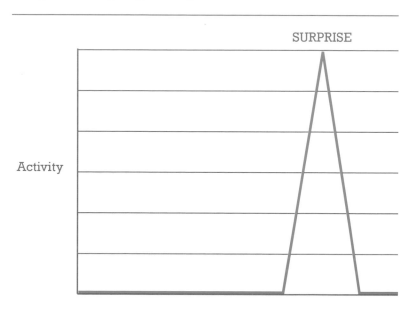

SURPRISE

Activity

Time

Pine tree saturation report:
Ottorino Respighi

Low

High

Rome

Concert etiquette flowchart

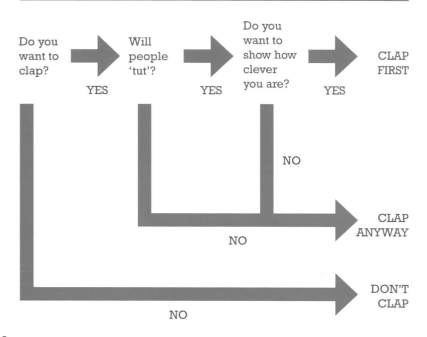

Do you want to clap? → **YES** → Will people 'tut'? → **YES** → Do you want to show how clever you are? → **YES** → CLAP FIRST

Do you want to show how clever you are? — **NO** → CLAP ANYWAY

Will people 'tut'? — **NO** → CLAP ANYWAY

Do you want to clap? — **NO** → DON'T CLAP

J. S. Bach's animal safety analysis

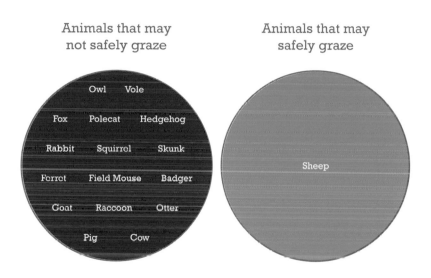

Animals that may not safely graze

Owl   Vole
Fox   Polecat   Hedgehog
Rabbit   Squirrel   Skunk
Ferret   Field Mouse   Badger
Goat   Raccoon   Otter
Pig   Cow

Animals that may safely graze

Sheep

Relationship between wakefulness and prettiness in ballet

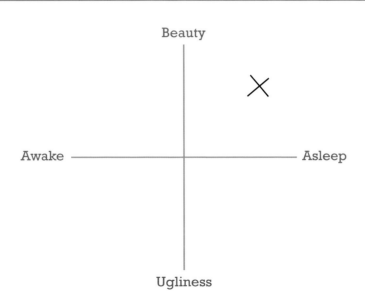

Distance from the song to the Moon

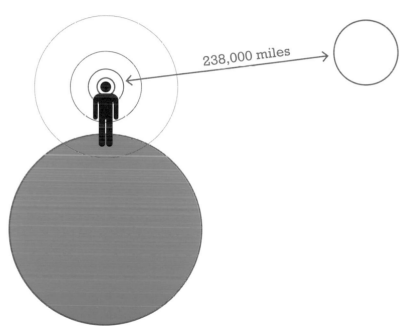

238,000 miles

Ratio of prosperity to level of fanfare

A rich man

:

A middle-class man

:

A common man

Temperature at which operatic arias have an effect on tiny hands

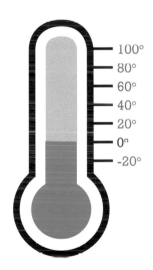

Analysis of coercion within brass section

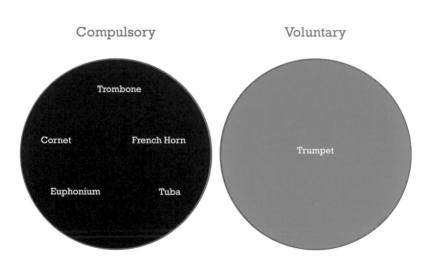

Compulsory

Trombone

Cornet   French Horn

Euphonium   Tuba

Voluntary

Trumpet

Units of alcohol contained in composer pairings

0
units

Brahms
and
Beethoven

0
units

Brahms
and
Mozart

0
units

Brahms
and
Bach

24
units

Brahms
and
Liszt

Chorus guide on forgetting lyrics to Karl Jenkins' Adiemus

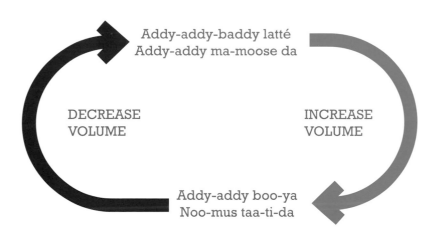

Addy-addy-baddy latté
Addy-addy ma-moose da

DECREASE
VOLUME

INCREASE
VOLUME

Addy-addy boo-ya
Noo-mus taa-ti-da

River/colour compatibility report

Zambezi	Red	☐
Danube	Blue	☑
Thames	Yellow	☐
Nile	Brown	☐
Rhine	Green	☐
Amazon	Pink	☐

Probable location of Peer Gynt within the Mountain King's Residence

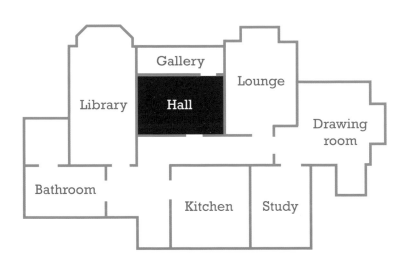

Delius's likely actions on hearing the first cuckoo in spring

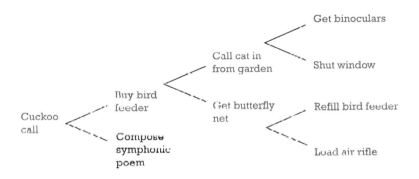

Cuckoo call
- Buy bird feeder
  - Call cat in from garden
    - Get binoculars
    - Shut window
  - Get butterfly net
    - Refill bird feeder
    - Load air rifle
- Compose symphonic poem

Populace assessment of sleeping habits during Turandot

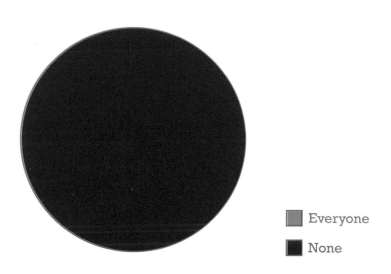

■ Everyone
■ None

Jaws: note count conversion table

NOTES	THREAT
One	Nil
Two	Minimal menace
Three	Cause for concern
Four	Definite threat
Multiple repeated notes	Seek help immediately
Unlimited repeated notes with horn melody	You're dead

Parting sentiments to Stromness

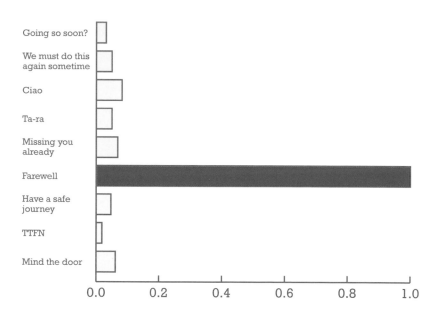

Mozart's symphonies with
a planetary attribution

Relative distances marched

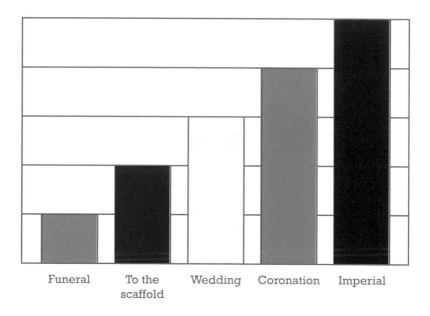

Funeral	To the scaffold	Wedding	Coronation	Imperial

Things Handel will/won't write music for

- [ ] Royal Halloween
- [ ] Royal Ascot
- [ ] Royal New Year's Eve
- [x] Royal Fireworks
- [ ] Royal Doulton
- [ ] Royal Baby

Composers' nocturnal productivity levels

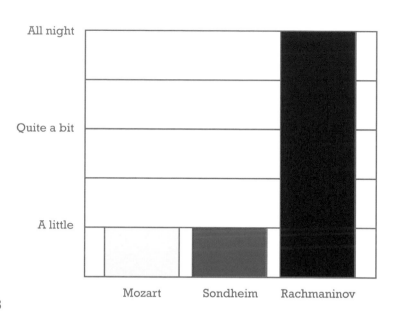

Relative importance of notes played by oboe on orchestral concert platform

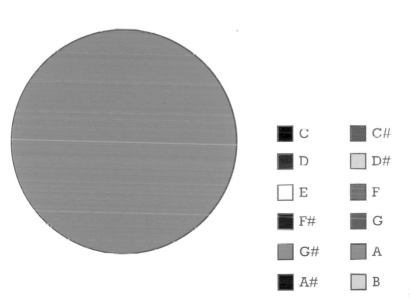

■ C		■ C#	
■ D		□ D#	
□ E		■ F	
■ F#		■ G	
■ G#		■ A	
■ A#		□ B	

Engagement level in instrument practice

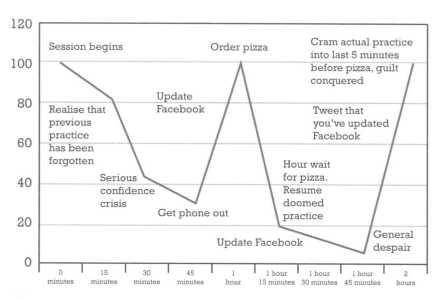

Beethoven/Saturday Night Fever compatibility analysis

Beethoven

Saturday Night Fever

Symphony No. 1
Symphony No. 2
Symphony No. 3
Symphony No. 4
Symphony No. 6
Symphony No. 7
Symphony No. 8
Symphony No. 9

Symphony No. 5

A Fifth of Beethoven

Stayin' Alive
How Deep Is Your Love
Night Fever
More Than A Woman
If I Can't Have You
Manhattan Skyline
Calypso Breakdown
Jive Talkin'

Quality assessment of Brahms' dwelling place

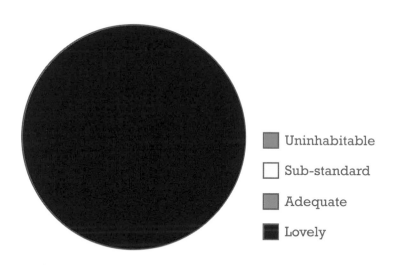

- Uninhabitable
- Sub-standard
- Adequate
- Lovely

Antonio Vivaldi's pizza choices

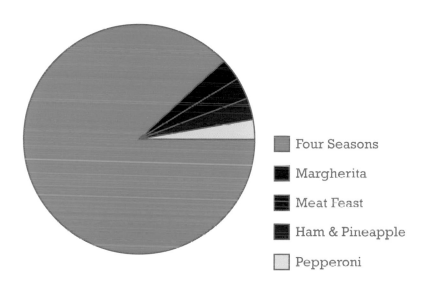

- Four Seasons
- Margherita
- Meat Feast
- Ham & Pineapple
- Pepperoni

Itinerary for Harold's tour of Europe

WEEKLY PLANNER

MONDAY
ROME

TUESDAY
BOLOGNA

WEDNESDAY
NAPLES

THURSDAY
MILAN

FRIDAY
TURIN

SATURDAY
GENOA

SUNDAY
FLORENCE

MONDAY
VENICE

TUESDAY
DEPART

Ornithological guide to best locations for twitching

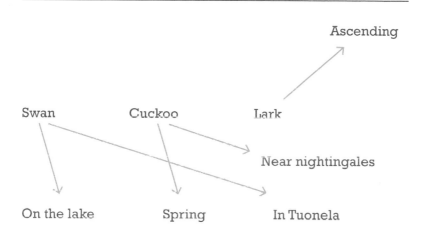

Ascending

Swan　　　　　Cuckoo　　　　　Lark

Near nightingales

On the lake　　　　Spring　　　　In Tuonela

Britannia's guide to success

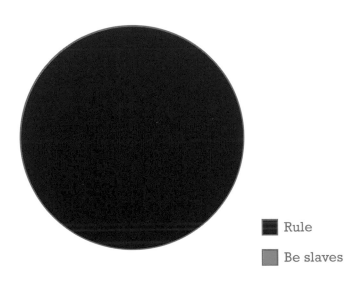

■ Rule

■ Be slaves

Entomology report on Shostakovich works

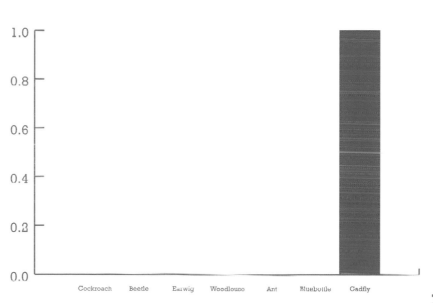

Physicists invited to build sandcastles with Philip Glass

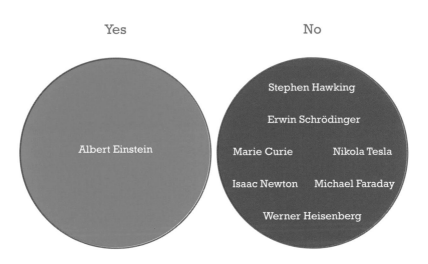

Yes

Albert Einstein

No

Stephen Hawking

Erwin Schrödinger

Marie Curie

Nikola Tesla

Isaac Newton

Michael Faraday

Werner Heisenberg

John Adams' preferred method of machine transport

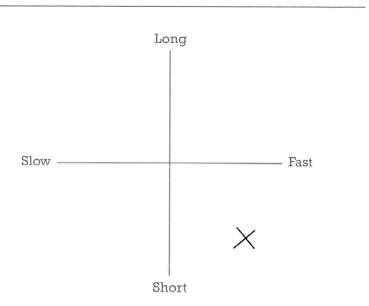

Suitable suites for Sibelius's abode

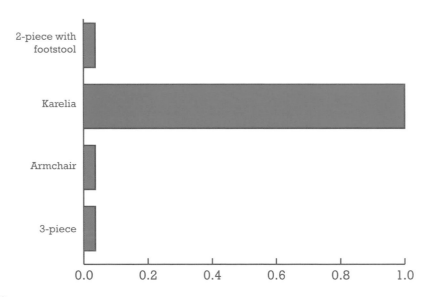

Number of Paganini pieces written for supermodels

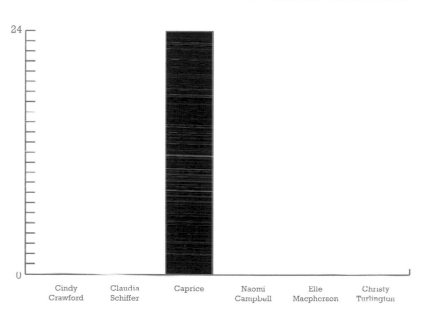

(repeat)

General ratios of sopranos, altos, tenors and basses

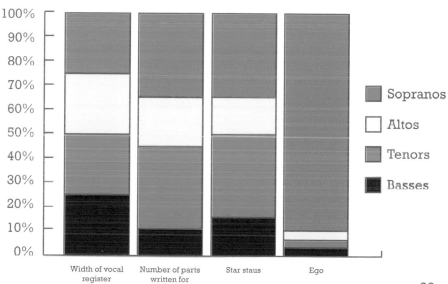

Job opportunities for Seville unemployed

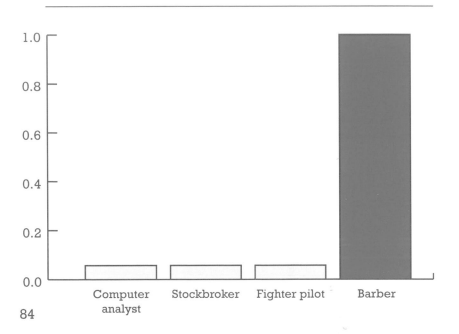

Aspects of arthropod life inspiring to Rimsky-Korsakov

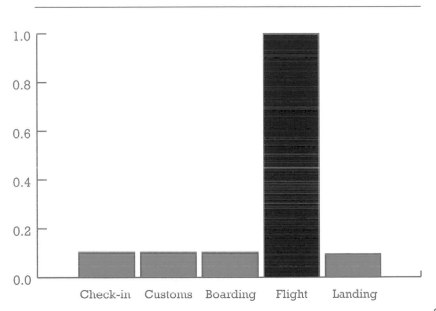

Guide to lengths of musical works (with comparisons)

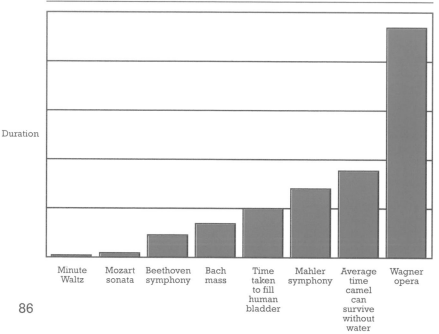

Duration

Minute Waltz | Mozart sonata | Beethoven symphony | Bach mass | Time taken to fill human bladder | Mahler symphony | Average time camel can survive without water | Wagner opera

Barber of Seville flowchart

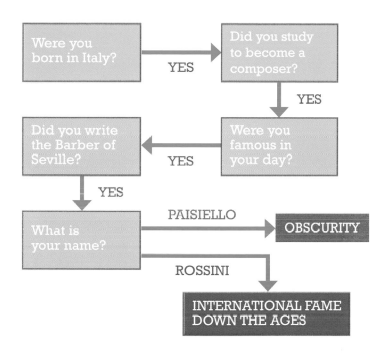

Favoured areas of both Chopin and Henry Ford (cross-correlated)

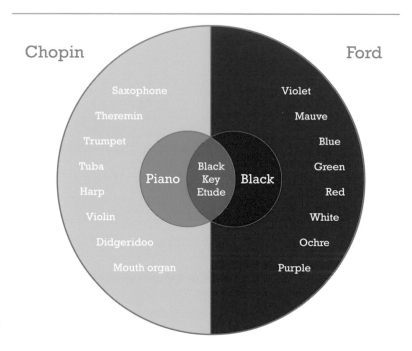

Chopin

Ford

Saxophone
Theremin
Trumpet
Tuba
Harp
Violin
Didgeridoo
Mouth organ

Piano

Black
Key
Etude

Black

Violet
Mauve
Blue
Green
Red
White
Ochre
Purple

Composing careers in the 19th century (using the Mendelssohns as an example)

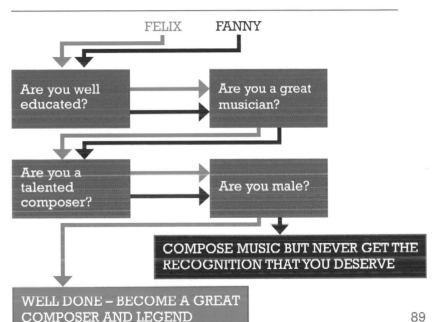

Winners and losers in Prokofiev's Peter and the Wolf

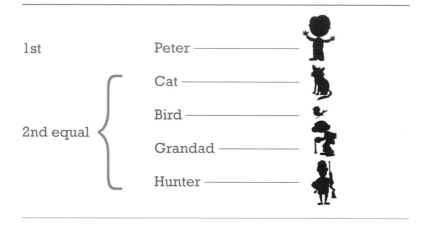

1st	Peter	
2nd equal	Cat	
	Bird	
	Grandad	
	Hunter	

Didn't finish	Wolf	
Didn't finish	Duck	(see above)

Most celebrated superheroes in classical music

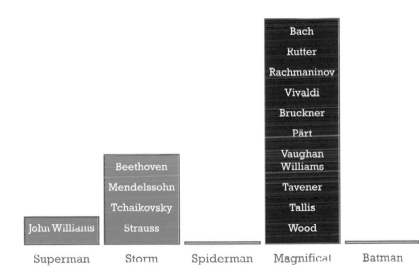

Superman	Storm	Spiderman	Magnificat	Batman
John Williams	Beethoven Mendelssohn Tchaikovsky Strauss		Bach Rutter Rachmaninov Vivaldi Bruckner Pärt Vaughan Williams Tavener Tallis Wood	

How to compose 'variations'

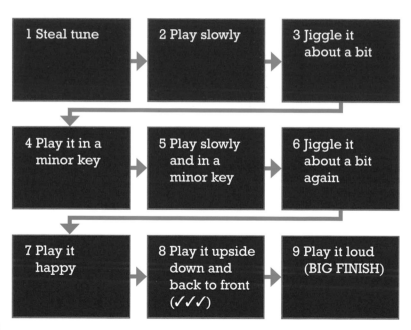

1 Steal tune

2 Play slowly

3 Jiggle it about a bit

4 Play it in a minor key

5 Play slowly and in a minor key

6 Jiggle it about a bit again

7 Play it happy

8 Play it upside down and back to front (✓✓✓)

9 Play it loud (BIG FINISH)

About the authors

Tim Lihoreau presents Classic FM's *More Music Breakfast* every weekday between 6 a.m. and 9 a.m. He has also written and produced a host of Classic FM programmes, winning a mantelpiece full of awards on both sides of the Atlantic.

Daniel Ross is content editor for ClassicFM.com. After studying music at Royal Holloway, University of London, he began his journalism career, writing extensively on music for a range of magazines and websites.

Darren Henley is managing director of Classic FM, where he has worked since the station's launch in 1992, writing 26 books about classical music along the way. He was appointed an OBE for services to music in the 2013 New Year Honours.

About Classic FM

Classic FM is part of Global, the media and entertainment company also behind Heart, Capital, Capital XTRA, LBC, Smooth, Xfm and Gold. Classic FM broadcasts the world's greatest music 24 hours a day across the UK on 100–102 FM, on DAB digital radio, online at www.ClassicFM.com, on Sky channel 0106, on Virgin Media channel 922 and on FreeSat channel 721, or direct to your mobile phone or tablet via our free Android and iOS apps.

As well as being able to listen online, you will find a host of interactive features about classical music, composers and musicians on our website ClassicFM.com. When we first turned on Classic FM's transmitters more than twenty years ago, we changed the face of classical music radio in the UK for ever. Two decades later, we are doing the same online. So, we've packed our website with up-to-the-minute classical music news, details of the latest recordings and upcoming concerts, big-name interviews and lots of information for anyone who wants to make a personal journey through the world of classical music.

Happy listening!

Index